HOW TO MAKE A PIUPIU

LEILANI RICKARD

To my granddaughters –
Anastasia, Nikita, Oksana
and Annuschka

A RAUPO BOOK
Published by the Penguin Group
Penguin Group (NZ), 67 Apollo Drive, Rosedale,
North Shore 0632, New Zealand (a division of Pearson New Zealand Ltd)
Penguin Group (USA) Inc., 375 Hudson Street,
New York, New York 10014, USA
Penguin Group (Canada), 90 Eglinton Avenue East, Suite 700, Toronto,
Ontario, M4P 2Y3, Canada (a division of Pearson Penguin Canada Inc.)
Penguin Books Ltd, 80 Strand, London, WC2R 0RL, England
Penguin Group (Australia), 250 Camberwell Road, Camberwell,
Victoria 3124, Australia (a division of Pearson Australia Group Pty Ltd)
Penguin Books India Pvt Ltd, 11, Community Centre,
Panchsheel Park, New Delhi – 110 017, India
Penguin Books (South Africa) (Pty) Ltd, 24 Sturdee Avenue,
Rosebank, Johannesburg 2196, South Africa

Penguin Books Ltd, Registered Offices: 80 Strand, London, WC2R 0RL, England

First published by Penguin Group (NZ), 2008
10 9 8 7 6 5 4 3 2

Text by IslandBridge
Cover design by Cheryl Rowe
Printed in China

ISBN13 9780143009450

A catalogue record for this book is available from the National Library of New Zealand.

www.penguin.co.nz

CONTENTS

ACKNOWLEDGEMENTS

Thank you to my granddaughters Anastasia, Nikita, Oksana and Annuschka who inspired me to write this book while sitting marking with flax. Anastasia said, 'Ma, my friends think it's cool that I know how to make a piupiu and other things out of flax, and I tell them that Ma has taught my sisters as well.' I'm pleased that my granddaughters are interested to take the time to learn and enjoy working with flax.

PREFACE

When I became one of the first permanent guides employed at Whakarewarewa in the early 1970s, part of my job was to weave tāniko headbands, bodices and other garments. We were required to wear traditional costume as our uniform throughout summer and winter. At the time, we were told that the modern piupiu was manufactured mainly as an entertainment accessory during the cultural renaissance of Māori people at the end of the nineteenth century. The use of Māori words set to European tunes captured the imagination of tourists to this country as a form of 'traditional' entertainment, rather than listening to the 'dirges' of more traditional Māori music. The first tourists arrived in the Rotorua district in the 1840s, so the link with tourism has been very long and a lot of innovative ideas about entertaining visitors have come from Rotorua. This suggests that perhaps the piupiu as we know it today came from this district. Not only that, the reintroduction of traditional dress such as the maro in kapa haka has been led by a Rotorua group, Te Matarae o Rehu. I would like to see a larger number of young people their age learning and experimenting with the medium.

I also now have one of my brothers, Chris, who helps me make piupiu. We now make piupiu full time for schools and kapa haka groups.

Māori women weaving piupiu and tāniko, c.1930.

Alexander Turnbull Library Te Puna Mātauranga o Aotearoa, PAColl-6075-11

INTRODUCTION

Unidentified Māori woman wearing piupiu, c.1900.

Photographer: W.H.T. Partington. Alexander Turnbull Library Te Puna Mātauranga o Aotearoa, 1/1-003116-G

The piupiu or flax kilt is a standard dress for Māori performing arts groups throughout Aotearoa New Zealand. It is an early twentieth century creation of a traditional Māori cloak or dress type called kākahu.

The piupiu reappeared when the revival of Māori culture was taking place at the turn of the twentieth century. Tourist demand for Māori entertainment led to the creation of a simple but eye-catching dress form that made a distinctive sound when worn. It still maintains its place as the number one dress accessory for performers, with the result that constant use has led to wear and tear on these garments.

The rustling sound that the piupiu makes adds to the overall effect when one is performing; but this would never have been used during the intertribal wars of yesteryear, as the rustling of the piupiu would easily be heard by the enemy.

This book is a step-by-step guide to making your own piupiu. Others may have slightly different methods but the result is the same.

Piupiu patterns exhibit regional differences: the East Coast style had finer cuts and the waistband was plaited. In the western style of piupiu, the muka dyed black was more prominent, and most had tāniko finger-woven waistbands, not unlike the borders on some of the korowai cloaks woven from plain muka, which had an elaborate border on the bottom.

The early entertainment costume for women consisted of a piupiu, of three-quarter length or longer, and a tāniko headband and bodice; and for men, a tāpeka instead of a bodice. These garments were made from flax fibre. However, because of the time-consuming nature of preparing and using traditional materials, Māori found that the European art of tapestry had similarities to tāniko, so new materials came into use. Unlike tāniko, tapestry is very stiff as a finished product, but it is much quicker to make, with the result that there are now very few groups that still wear the tāniko bodices and headbands.

The piupiu patterns that have been used in the past are simply amazing, but are also very time-consuming to make, and the pressure to use good flax leads to over-cutting of the flax bush, with no recuperation time for the plant. This, in turn, leads to poor quality fibre and length.

Korirangi is the pattern most commonly used for piupiu and there are many variations of it. You can make the sections in between each cut wider or narrower, or vary the number of cuts.

You have to be very careful when scraping the fine cuts. If you slip from one cut to another, you will only notice the mistake later after the piupiu is dyed. It will be very noticeable and should not be used. If you are a beginner, it is best to keep the cuts wide at first so they are manageable. As you progress, finer cuts can be made. Most people have no idea how labour-intensive piupiu-making is, but whether the piupiu is large or small, the length and sequence of the process remains the same.

There seems to be interest in learning tāniko and the making of korowai with both traditional and modern materials, but using traditional techniques. Customary methods are being kept alive not only by Māori but by people of all nationalities, and large numbers are now wanting to learn how to make piupiu, kete (bags) and piupiu whāriki (mats). The same can be said for other weavers, using traditional and contemporary mixes and their own ideas, going back to older style garments but utilising brighter colours.

MATERIALS

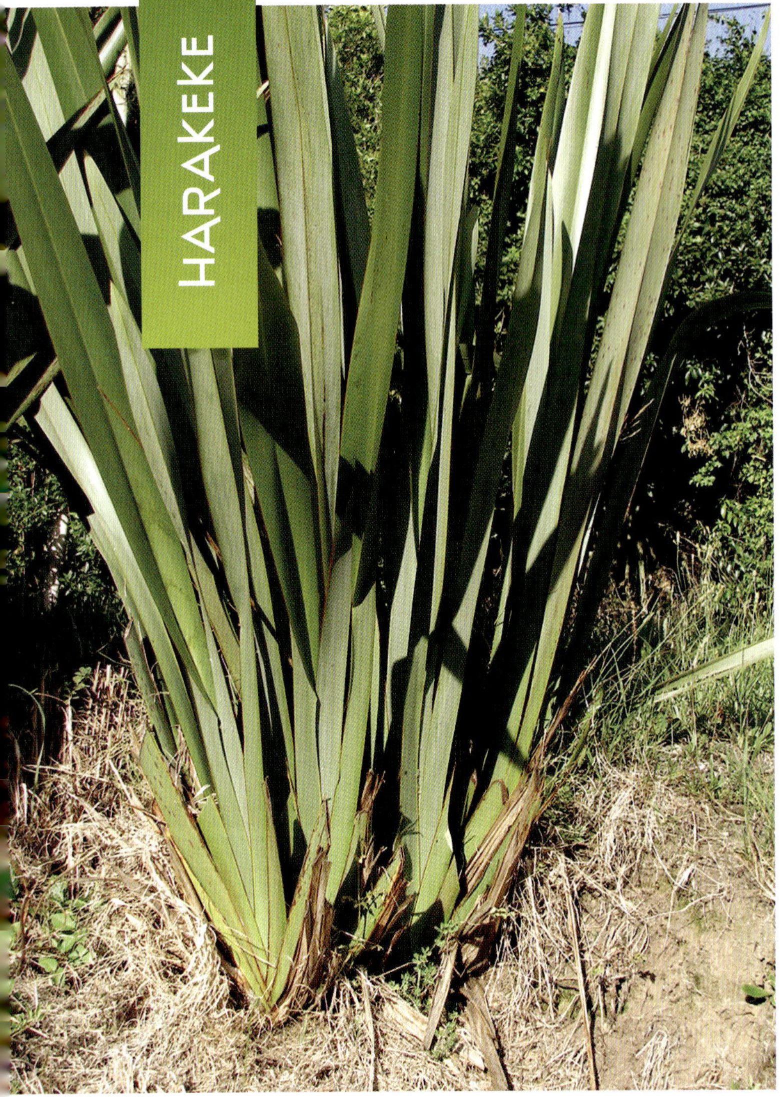

HARAKEKE

Harakeke or flax (*Phormium tenax*), as it is commonly known, is a versatile and hardy plant which grows best in swampy areas. Clothing was one of the many uses made of flax. It was used for both piupiu and sandals, as well as for food containers, sleeping mats, bird snares, splints, and sewing wounds or sails.

The whakapapa or genealogy of the flax shows the habitat that best suits this plant.

Ra = Arohirohi
|
Marikoriko = Tiki
|
Pakoti = Tane
|
Pa = Harakeke

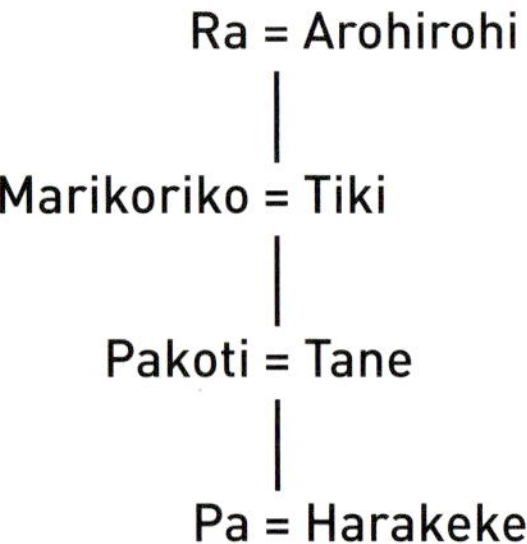

Harakeke grows as a series of fans comprised of eight to ten blades, with numerous fans making up a flax bush. The number of blades in a fan of flax depends on whether or not the plant has been cut before. There will be more blades on a flax bush that has not been worked before, however, some bushes need to be cleaned right back to start from scratch especially if the blades show speckled brown spotting.

The rito of the harakeke is the small central blade of the fan, which to Māori represents the next generation of flax. The two blades closest to the rito are the awhi rito or parents, the next two blades are the grandparents, and so on.

It is important to keep your flax plant healthy. To achieve this, keep cutting all the excess blades back to the three central blades. This helps strengthen the fibre in the plant.

For beginners, it is important to know how to choose the correct flax bush and, when making piupiu, it is necessary to select flax that has a high fibre content. To select a good flax bush, cut a single blade of flax then strip the outer edges, scour the blade in the middle and run the straight edge of a mussel shell either side of the blade. The fibre exposed by the mussel shell scraping should be thick. If the fibre is thin, find another blade to test.

It is a matter of trial and error to find a good flax bush. It is also one of the reasons why weavers jealously guard their patches, as good muka flax is hard to find. Run tests of a few samples until you find a good crop of flax. The photograph shows a typical blade that can be used.

A flax blade consists of a leaf with a seam running through the entire length and different coloured outer edges. This is an indication of what type of flax to look for when selecting a bush to use. When selecting a flax bush to use for your piupiu, look for blades with a black edge as this type contains high fibre and grows tall. Bear in mind, though, that you can often find high-fibre flax bushes without black edges.

The flax blade has two distinct sides:

- a shiny inner side, as shown in the top photograph on the left,
- and a dull outer surface, as shown in the bottom photograph on the left.

Like all plants, harakeke can be infected by a number of parasites. The flax weevil can grow up to 25 mm long, sucking sap from the leaves and causing yellow discolouration. They form white woolly patches or tubes on the underside of the leaves. After cleaning a flax bush, take all the rubbish away from the plant to prevent re-infection.

Pattern board

Use a 10 cm x 90 cm hardwood board made from a hard native timber to mark the pattern on. It is not recommended to use a soft wood board as you could probably only mark five bundles before cutting through the flax blade and wasting flax. When this happens it is advisable to remark a new board. Pattern boards made from hard native timbers such as black maire are especially durable and will last a lot longer before you have to clean the board and remark the pattern.

Mussel shell

The straight edge of a mussel shell is used to scrape the flax blade and expose the muka. Do not use a cultivated shell as these are very weak and break easily. A shell should last five years or more if it is looked after. It takes a lot of scraping to blunt a mussel shell, but when it does become blunt, use sandpaper to sharpen the shell. Use a shell that fits comfortably into the palm of the hand, as scraping an entire piupiu can take at least 3 to 4 hours. To prevent blistering your hands, especially when first learning, it is a good idea to use plasters on the hand where the shell applies the most pressure.

Craft knife

The sharp edge of a mussel shell was originally used for marking the pattern, but modern weavers use a craft knife (or Stanley knife) instead. Blunt the knife blade on concrete first so as to prevent cutting through the flax blade. A typical craft knife blade can last for around 180 piupiu. You will know when to change the blade when scraping the flax becomes more difficult.

Large capacity boiler or stockpot

Use a large copper or a purpose-built boiler to boil prepared flax, instead of submerging the flax in a natural thermal spring. A suitable boiler will be able to hold 10 bundles of flax at one time. If you are only making small quantities of piupiu at one time, use a jampan or a large pot, which you can obtain from a hardware store, for boiling and also for cooking the mānuka for the waiwai (see page 20), as part of the dyeing process.

Seaming twine

Seaming twine or binder twine is waste flax that has been treated in flaxmills. It used to be readily available; but now it is almost impossible to find. String nowadays comes from China, and is sold in $2 shops. Don't use plastic string, as it is not easy to work with and will not take the natural dyes like string does.

Waiwai

The waiwai acts as a mordant or fixer, as the first part of the dyeing process and for rinsing the flax. It is a brew traditionally created from the bark, branches and leaves of mānuka, tawhero or tutu plants.

Paru

Paru is decomposed vegetation found underwater in the banks of slow-moving streams or ponds. The muddy substance is thick and slimy with an unusual, potent smell and when it has been sitting for a while it bubbles as it ferments. It is used to give the piupiu colour, and is used in the second phase of the dyeing process. Give it a good stir before using. Always add the waiwai used for rinsing the flax back into the paru otherwise it will eventually dry up. Not all streams and ponds will have paru, and just like good sources of flax their locations tend to be closely guarded secrets.

METHODS

CUTTING

If the flax bush has not been cut before, it will have fans consisting of seven to nine blades. Make sure the blades are clean, without any specks or yellowing. Clean flax will replenish itself quickly if kept clean and tidy following cutting, and will regenerate at 3 to 6 month intervals. When planting flax, split the bushes to allow them to grow better, and plant them in groups of 3 to 4 fans so that they will grow faster. The photograph shows well-planted flax bushes.

For safety's sake, do not cut flax when it is raining as the blades can become slippery and dangerous to handle. Traditionally, women were prohibited from cutting flax while going through their menstrual cycle – as with many cultures women were considered taboo at this time and only resumed work when their cycle was finished. Today this restriction is not emphasised, although I have been told that if you are gathering or dyeing piupiu when you have your cycle then the mud you're using will not be in the same place next time or be discoloured.

Only cut what you are capable of working with so that the flax blades do not dry out and become unusable. As you gain experience at marking and scraping, the amount of flax you cut will increase.

When cutting flax during the winter, flax can last up to a week if it is kept out of the sun and in a cool place. During summer, however, flax will last two days once cut and can be kept only two days, under a damp cloth or towel, before it must be worked on.

Cutting – Step 1

Cut the blades near the base of the bush – this leaves it tidy. Always move in a circular direction around the outer edge of the bush when cutting flax and gradually make your way towards the centre.

Do not cut the blade up high as this creates sharp points and makes it difficult when cutting further into the centre of the bush.

Tie blades in bundles of 10 pairs. This makes it easier to calculate the number of bundles per waist size.

Cutting – Step 2

Once the blades have been stripped (see pages 29–31) and if you are not going to mark the flax right away, keep them under a damp cloth or towel for up to 3 to 4 days. The blades must be scraped within this time or they will discolour. Once the flax has been scraped and put into bundles, boil it straightaway (see *Boiling* pages 41–42). If left to become brown the flax will be of no use.

Step 1

Fold the blade of flax in half (as shown in the top photograph) and use your thumbnail to strip down both edges of the blade (as shown in the bottom photograph). To give a workable width it is better to strip the blade a little wider than you require. You can always strip a little more off the blade if you find it is too wide and in danger of splitting. Begin by using standard widths of 2 cm.

Stripping – Step 2

Continue to strip down to the white fleshy part near the stalk, then cut with scissors just above the white flesh.

If the blade of flax is too wide it may split, so ensure that you have a standard size that feels comfortable in your hand.

Stripping – Step 3

The more flax you strip, the faster you become. The photograph shows a pair of stripped blades of the approximate width required.

Step 1

Mark your pattern on to the marking board with a dark pencil or black felt pen (see *Patterns* on pages 45–49).

Marking – Step 2

Place a thumbtack at the end of the marking board to act as a stopper for the blade of flax when you begin marking. The bottom of the piupiu is placed against the tack when marking.

Marking – Step 3

Place your blade of flax with the dull side facing up. Ensure that the right amount of pressure is applied when using the Stanley knife so that the knife does not sever the blade. Remember you are only marking the blade, not cutting it.

Marking – Step 4

The pressure required should be enough to cut the outer layer, but not to sever the muka. Over time, you will soon find the right pressure.

How to use a mussel shell – Step 1

Use a mussel shell that fits comfortably into the palm of the hand. There is a right- and left-handed shell so use whichever is appropriate. Place the blade to be scraped with the shiny side facing upwards.

How to use a mussel shell – Step 2

A beginner will find that there is a lot of fluffy fibre (para) left when you scrape over the pattern marks. This is caused by scraping in the same spot too many times and will improve with time. Less para is better, as it all needs to be removed so that the dye can take. Hold the shell in one hand and, using the thumb, apply downward pressure on to the blade (top left). This will loosen the dark underside (top right) of the pattern.

How to use a mussel shell – Step 3

Once you have gone down the blade and exposed the fibres, turn the blade over to the dull side and clip the loose pieces of outer skin.

How to use a mussel shell – Step 4

Using the other hand as a guide, move the blade along the entire length, scraping as you go. When you arrive at the tapered part of the flax, use one complete motion to expose the fibre.

How to use a mussel shell – Step 5

The filmy substance that covers the fibre is called para and acts as waterproofing. This is why the para must be removed in order for the dyeing process to work. If the flax is marked correctly there should be no problem removing the para.

BOILING

Boil the flax within 48 hours of scraping it in winter or within 24 hours in summer. If you have no access to a boiling pool such as those found in the Rotorua region, use a large stock-pot that can take two to three bundles at a time. Ensure the flax is totally submerged in the boiling water, but do not submerge the top part of any blades from which the waistband will be woven (see *Finishing* pages 51–61), as water in the fibre will drip to the bottom of the blade and cause the fibre to become waterlogged. Submerge the green part of the blade only. Waterlogged fibre cannot be fixed by dry heat, but sometimes a blow fan that circulates warm air will help.

Continue to boil for three to four minutes, remove and shake off the excess water outdoors. Flax retains a lot of water so after boiling hang the blades on a clothesline or in a well ventilated area, preferably with a breeze, to dry thoroughly. Hang by a fire in winter to take the moisture out of the blades.

Within 24 hours the flax will curl into tubes. It is important to check the blades and separate them so they do not roll into one another. If left for too long the blades will split when you are trying to separate them, so once they are boiled, check them every day until they have completely curled. Leave the tubes until they have dried to a creamy white colour and then they can be attached to the waistband and left to dry. At this stage, the flax is ready for dyeing.

A piupiu and tāniko weaving, Koriniti, Whanganui River, 1921.

Alexander Turnbull Library Te Puna Mātauranga o Aotearoa, PA1-q-257-43-4

PATTERNS

There are numerous patterns that can be incorporated in piupiu-making, and some have at least four different cuts. The different cut and marked bundles should be kept in separate piles in order to get the pattern correct. If an incorrectly cut strand is used at the beginning, the piupiu will have to be pulled apart and begun again, so it is always a good idea to check the pattern as the piupiu is being put together.

Some people create their own patterns, and many kapa haka groups may request a specific pattern, so when making piupiu in bulk it is important to select a pattern that can be easily adjusted to weaving for different waist sizes.

While you are learning, it is best to stay with the korirangi (shining cuckoo) pattern described opposite, which is muka exposed at intervals to give a striped effect. The korirangi pattern is a plain stripe: for piupiu worn by men this usually involves around 8 to 9 cuts; for piupiu worn by women there should be around 13 to 14 cuts. Once you have mastered this, you can move to more complicated patterns.

In a man's piupiu there are usually around 8 or 9 cuts, but you can make the cuts really fine and have up to 15 cuts.

In women's piupiu, there are usually 13 or 14 cuts but I have made a 26 cm length woman's piupiu with 19 very fine cuts.

Korirangi – Step 1

The first line is marked 3 cm from where the thumbtack has been placed in the marking board. A 2 cm gap to the next cut will form the first marking.

Korirangi – Step 2

Leave a space of 3.5 cm then repeat the marking – this will produce the korirangi pattern. For a woman's piupiu of 25 to 26 cm in length, around 13 to 14 cuts are sufficient. You can make them finer or use more cuts – it is entirely up to you. For a man's piupiu there are normally at least 8 to 9 cuts.

When making more complicated patterns you could have anything up to 4 to 5 cuts, but of different lengths. Care must be taken when assembling your piupiu that they are in the correct sequence or a consistent pattern will not appear.

It is best to mark all the blades immediately. If you cannot scrape the blades straightaway, cover them with a damp cloth but do not leave them longer than 3 days or the flax will discolour and all the previous hard work will be wasted.

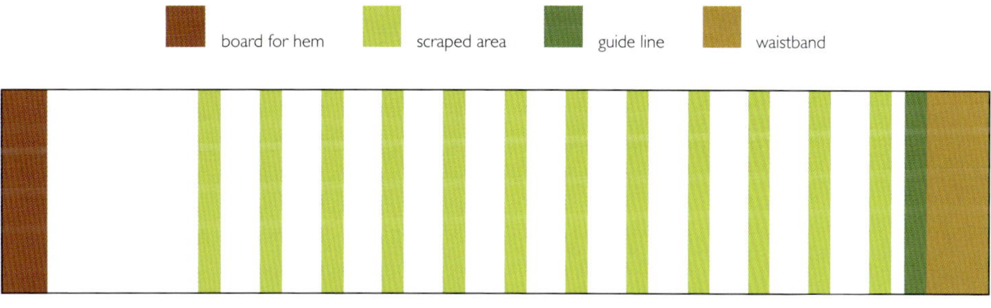

Pattern board for korirangi design

Above

Mūmū pattern — black with korirangi top and bottom of block

Right

Poutama steps — stepped pattern

Above

Tuhourangi pattern — smaller cuts, create diagonal or diamond pattern

Right

A variant on the korirangi pattern using smaller cuts

FINISHING

Here are the steps involved in making the cord to weave the waistband.

Miro – Step 1

Once the blades have been scraped, take two blades of flax and place the shiny sides back to back. At the top of the blade separate the exposed fibres evenly into two strands.

Miro – Step 2

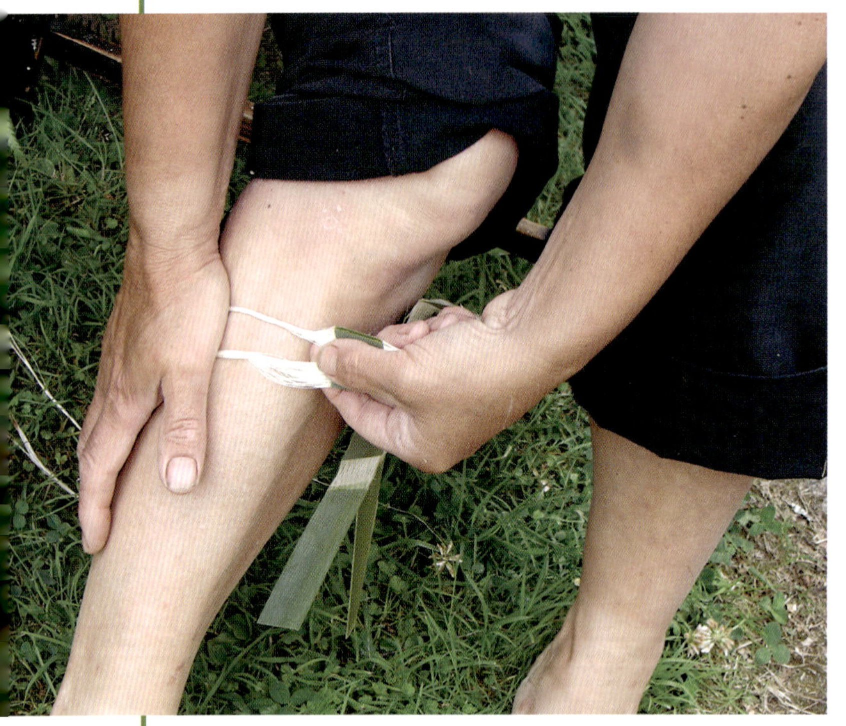

Hold the blades in the left hand and with the palm of the right hand roll the fibres down the side of your bare leg until the top strands of fibre roll over the bottom strands.

Miro – Step 3

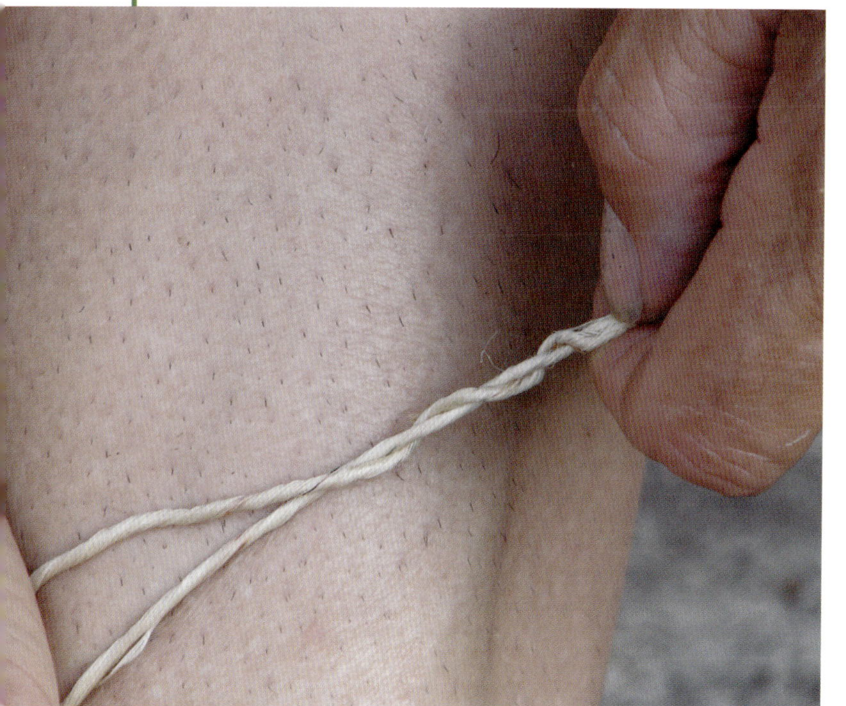

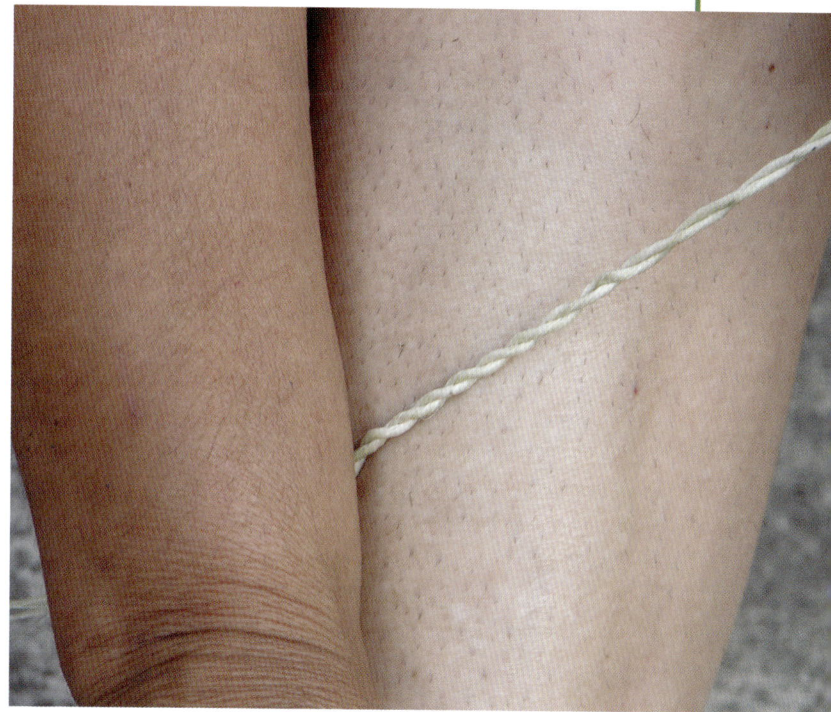

Roll the palm of the hand back up the leg and the strands will interlock to make a cord which will later be woven into the waistband. The fibre should be nice and thick, as the waistband needs to be at least 4 to 5 cm wide. The thicker the muka the longer the piupiu will last.

Miro – Step 4

Put the flax into bundles of five and tie two of these together to maker one bundle of ten pairs ready to be boiled (see *Boiling* pages 65–66).

An example method for weaving a waistband for an 86 cm waist follows.

NB: For larger waists, weave with 8 or 10 strands instead of 6. The waistband will be wider.

Step 1

Take four strands of seaming twine, each 3.86 m in length. Align the four strands and tie a knot 1.5 m from each end.

Whatu – Step 2

Separate the seaming twine into two groups, 2 up and 2 down.

Whatu – Step 3

Take one of the muka strands and lay it on the bottom 2 strands of seaming twine. Bring the top 2 strands of twine over the top of the muka to secure the muka in place.

Whatu – Step 4

Repeat Step 3 until 86 cm has been reached and tie a knot at the end of the plaited band. Tie all the blades together into a single unit to complete.

You are now ready to weave your waistband. Waistbands can be as wide as the length of the muka strands allow, so the more experienced you become, the wider the waistband will be.

Step 1

Take 6 strands of muka fibre. Fold the first strand of muka over the second strand and work until you have 2 strands of muka to one side, 2 strands to the top of the string and 2 strands below.

Step 2

Take the first strand forward over the next. Bring one strand back and then one forward and repeat the process until the end. Tuck the last strand around towards the back of the piupiu.

FASHIONING THE WAISTBAND

To ensure the waistband of the piupiu is nice and flat:

- Use muka of equal thickness.
- Do not weave the waistband too tight.

Step 1

Take three strands and fold the first strand over the top of the others until you have three pieces of muka to weave the back of your piupiu then tuck the third strand under. Continue this procedure to the end of your piupiu.

Step 2

Divide the strands and the string into equal amounts and plait this back to make your waistband. To plait, fold the first strand over the second strand, then position the third strand over the first before folding the second strand back over the third strand so that it lies to your left. Then pick up your fourth strand and position over the second strand before folding the third strand back to lie to your left. Repeat.

Step 3

Trim back leaving about 4 cm of muka. If your weaving is too tight, the waistband will be wavy and not flat, but this will improve with practice. If you have to add some extra twine because your strands are too short, cut some extra strands of twine and use scissors to push the string into the very end of the muka part of the waistband. Then just divide the string and plait your string.

If you misjudge the amount of string necessary for the handles of your piupiu, they will be too short, so to make them long enough, insert some strings at the end of the waistband (muka part) and plait. When properly finished, the piupiu should meet evenly and neatly at the back.

I prefer dyeing the traditional way as there are not so many things that can go wrong if you stick to those methods. My auntie Katie Whareauitu always said if you have been taught the traditional way and you try to take shortcuts, it won't work and you will end up ruining your work.

Waiwai

The waiwai acts as a mordant or a fixer for the next part of the dyeing process, which uses paru or swamp mud.

Waiwai – Step 1

Use a large copper or a purpose-built boiler and fill with cold water up to around 10 cm from the top: a 53 cm x 58 cm pot will dye 10 piupiu. Strip the bark, branches and leaves of mānuka, tawhero or tutu into small pieces and place into the boiler. Older trees are preferred, especially if they have berries as they contain oils which make the solution stronger. If these are not available use tea bags; however, for 10 piupiu you would need between 400 to 500 tea bags! The longer you brew them the better, so when it becomes a really dark brown it is ready. Once the brew is brought to the boil and cooled, put the piupiu in for 40 minutes. If the solution is left unused for a few days, it will need to be warmed before putting in the piupiu.

Waiwai – Step 2

Remove the piupiu from the waiwai and rinse with cold water before drying. If you do not rinse the piupiu at this point, when it is put into the paru it will stick to the areas you have not exposed and will have to be cleaned.

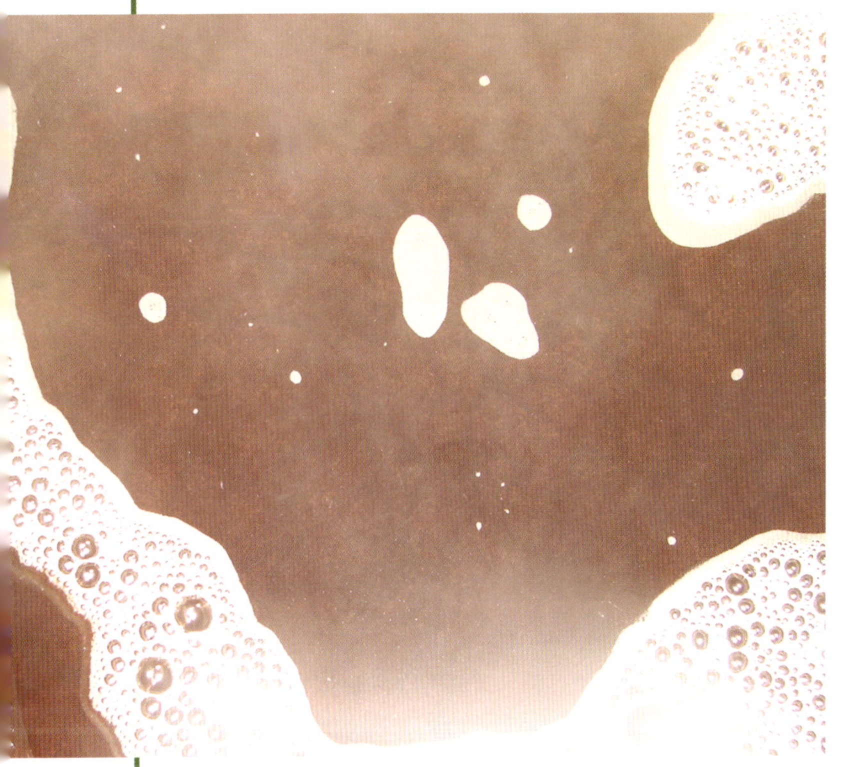

Waiwai

Step 3

Once the first piupiu has been dyed, top up the waiwai with more water and fresh mānuka and repeat the process. This waiwai will last for about a week before a fresh batch will need to be made. You will be able to tell if the waiwai is too weak by the colour of your piupiu. Strengthen the waiwai by adding mānuka or whatever you have available.

If the waiwai is not dark or strong enough when the piupiu is placed into the paru, the piupiu will come out a grey colour instead of black. If this happens, the whole dyeing process has to be repeated.

Step 4

The piupiu must be dried immediately after it has been in the waiwai and before putting it in the paru. Drying should be done outdoors on a fine day – drying naturally is far better for the blades as they will not become brittle. Lay the piupiu on a grassed area or garage floor to drain off excess water and hang on a clothes line in the wind to finish drying. If the weather conditions are not right at the time, a fan or a gas heater can be used.

Paru

This is decomposed vegetation or swamp mud found in the banks of slow-moving streams and ponds. It is not visible from the surface of the water and must be felt with the hands by scouring the bottom of the stream or pond. If you don't have access to paru there are commercial dyes you can use, but you have to be very careful as they can ruin a piupiu if you have not used them before.

If making a large number of piupiu, the paru in the 'rinsing waiwai' can be drained off after a few days and put back into the paru tub.

According to tradition, women who are menstruating should not be near the mud or be dyeing, nor should they gather the mud. Tubs or containers with paru should be kept away from the residence. Be selective as to who you tell where you gather from to ensure the mud is looked after.

Step 1

An old bathtub is ideal to use. It should be at least half filled with paru and mixed with some waiwai. This will start working like yeast. If the tub has previously been used with paru and been left sitting for some months, add two buckets of waiwai and mix into the mud. Leave to work for about three hours before using the mud for dyeing piupiu. Always keep the paru tub covered.

Paru – Step 2

Piupiu should be laid flat, one at a time in the paru, and six piupiu should fit totally immersed in the tub of mud. Leave for 45 minutes.

Paru – Step 3

Use gloves when taking the piupiu out of the mud and run your hands down the piupiu to wipe off as much mud as possible back into the tub.

Paru – Step 4

Rinse the piupiu in a large plastic bin which is half filled with waiwai, then use a hose to rinse off the remaining mud.

Paru – Step 5

Repeat the same drying method as for the waiwai process (see pages 65–69). It is best to drain the material on grass before hanging on a line to dry completely, as waterlogging leaves dark marks on the blades which will not fade. When the piupiu is completely dry and the loose fibres have been trimmed, place the piupiu in a stocking or an onion bag to keep it tidy. Always store piupiu in a dry area, for example, a hotwater cupboard.

STORAGE AND CARE

The lifespan of a piupiu depends on how often it is worn: if it is worn every day, it will probably need to be replaced from time to time, especially after kapa haka where there is constant movement of the piupiu. When men are performing the haka, they are continually slapping their hands on to the blades of the piupiu, which causes wear and tear. Anyone wearing the garment can care for their piupiu by ensuring they separate the blades of the piupiu before sitting down, so that the blades do not split.

When the piupiu are not in use, keep them in a stocking and in dry storage, which will give them a life of 5 to 10 years.

GALLERY

KAHUKARE

The piupiu production process

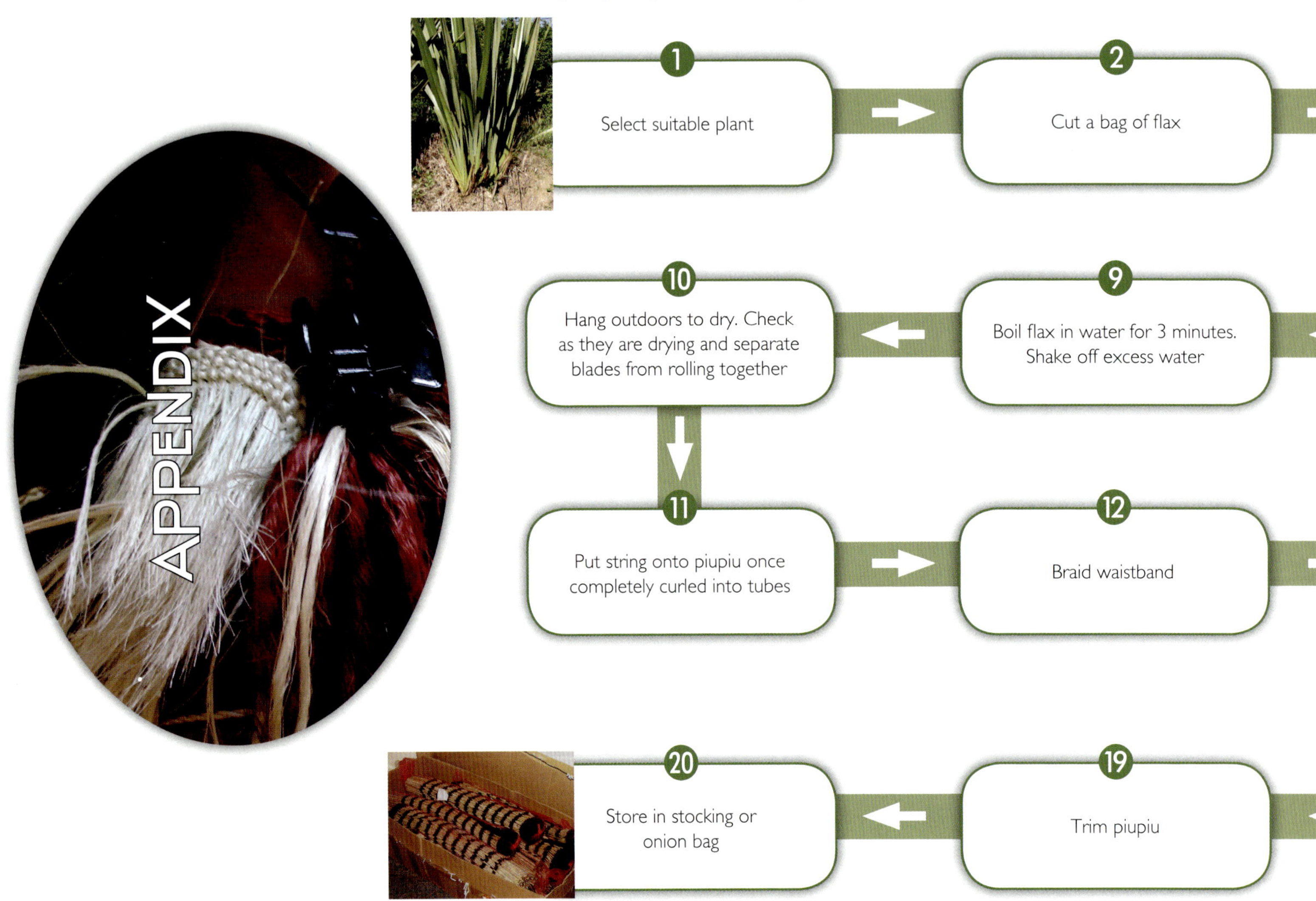

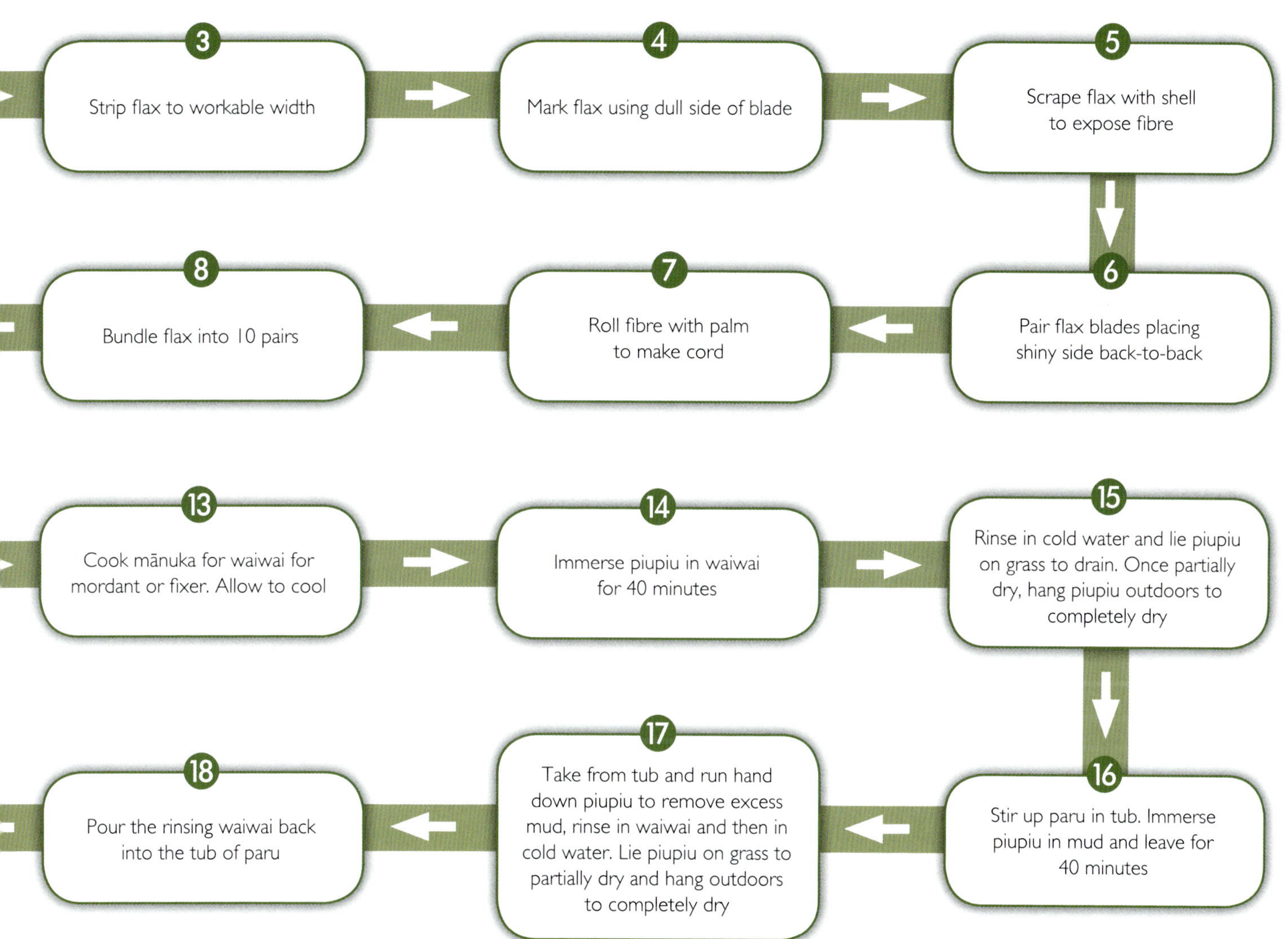
3
Strip flax to workable width
4
Mark flax using dull side of blade
5
Scrape flax with shell to expose fibre
6
Pair flax blades placing shiny side back-to-back
7
Roll fibre with palm to make cord
8
Bundle flax into 10 pairs
13
Cook mānuka for waiwai for mordant or fixer. Allow to cool
14
Immerse piupiu in waiwai for 40 minutes
15
Rinse in cold water and lie piupiu on grass to drain. Once partially dry, hang piupiu outdoors to completely dry
16
Stir up paru in tub. Immerse piupiu in mud and leave for 40 minutes
17
Take from tub and run hand down piupiu to remove excess mud, rinse in waiwai and then in cold water. Lie piupiu on grass to partially dry and hang outdoors to completely dry
18
Pour the rinsing waiwai back into the tub of paru

awhirito	embrace, support
harakeke	flax *Phormium tenax*
kākahu	traditional dress
kapa haka	dance procession
kete	basket, bag
korirangi	fine black and white pattern
korowai	mantle
maire	tree *Nestegis cunninghamii*
mānuka	tea tree *Leptosperum scoparium*
maro	girdle or loincloth
miro	twist thread, brown pine *Prumnopitys ferruginea*
muka	flax fibre
mūmū	block pattern
paru	swamp mud
piupiu	flax skirt
poutama	stairway pattern
rito	heart of plant
tāniko	braid, tapestry or embroidered border
tāpeka	sash worn by men
tawhero (whero)	tree *Quintinia serrata*
Tuhourangi	Te Arawa subtribe
tutu	shrub *Coriaria arborea*
waiwai	fixer for dye
whakapapa	genealogy
whāriki	woven mat
whatu	weave

'Flax: the enduring fibre' in *New Zealand Geographic*, 42 April/June 1999.

Hopa, N. *The Art of Piupiu Making*. Reed Publishing, Auckland, 1971.

Mead, H.M. *Te Whatu Tāniko : Taniko Weaving Technique and Tradition.* Reed Publishing: Auckland, 1999.

Pendergrast, M. *Fun with Flax*. Reed Publishing: Auckland, 1987.

Pendergrast, M. *Ka tahi: Maori Fibre Technique*. Reed Publishing, Auckland, 2005.

Scheele, S. *Harakeke: the Rene Orchiston Collection.* DSIR: Havelock North, 1988.

INDEX

Living at Okere Falls, Rotorua, and surrounded by flax bushes, I am fortunate to have a family who have put up with flax in different stages for piupiu around the house. Working on a ground sheet to keep the mess in one area is not always possible; quite often paru is from one end of the house to the other. In the summer I use the garage for drying, whereas winter is when the lounge becomes a Chinese laundry with piupiu hanging everywhere. I do get reprimanded now and again when the piupiu are blocking the television – clothes airers are ideal but they take up space!

I can't imagine not working with flax in one way or another. I am now experimenting with garments woven out of muka and have produced some creations for the Wearable Arts show in Rotorua. I am now busier with flax than ever before. Piupiu is my main daily work, extracting fibre in between to make other creations.